CALM MOM

TIPS AND TRICKS TO STOP YELLING, STAY CALM, AND RAISE HAPPY, HEALTHY KIDS

DR. CHRISTINE HARKNESS

Difference Press

Washington, DC, USA

Published 2021

Cover design: Jennifer Stimson

Editing: Natasa Smirnov

Author's photo courtesy of: Jennifer Thomas

ADVANCE PRAISE

"I relate to Dr. Christine Harkness's examples in *Calm Mom*. She aids us with practical applications. The layout of her chapters is clear, and the 'Try It Now' sections help reinforce her points of encouragement. I'm really thankful for *Calm Mom* and Dr. Christine Harkness."

— AMY, MOM

"A great read for everyone! Dr. Christine Harkness offers clear and precise principles. The 'Try It Now' sections are practical and easy to apply. Her real-life examples allow you to really connect with the book."

— TAMARA, EDUCATOR AND MOM

"A wonderful parenting one-stop shop without all the 'fluff.' The techniques were easy to understand and included great practice activities to help me realize that I, too, can do hard things! Parenting can be hard and messy, but this book definitely gives me the tools to make it easier and more intentional!"

— LAURA, AUTISM CONSULTANT AND MOM

CONTENTS

This book is dedicated to Mary and Martha who taught me the most about being a parent, to Barb and Dave who modeled unconditional love, and to all the parents who trusted me to care for your children.

Thank you.

1

I'M WORKING HARD BUT AM I WORKING SMART?

"If I have the belief that I can do it, I shall surely acquire the capacity to do it even if I may not have it at the beginning."

— GANDHI

Cara glances over her laptop and sees her son Luke come into the living room where she's been working on an email to her boss. She asked Luke to play with his younger sister in the playroom, but from the squeezed lips, marching legs, and the tight hug around his box of Legos, she's guessing that did not go so well. She takes a deep breath and mumbles under her breath, "Just finish the sentence, Cara, focus."

Seconds later, in comes Sarah with her crayons and some paper. Luke gives her the eye.

"You can't be here!"

"I can too."

"Sit far away from me!"

Cara hits send. Okay, back to momming. Luke and Sarah are already in the middle of a fight. Let them work it out, don't be a referee, they need to learn to do this.

"Mommmmmm! Did you see what she did? Mommmmm!" Luke screams.

"No, Luke, I didn't see. I know I asked you to play nicely with your sister in the playroom – I'm sure not seeing that, either."

Cara moves to the kitchen to make some snacks. She's still keeping an eye on Luke and Sarah, while she uses cookie cutters to turn the veggies and cheese into an art display. Meanwhile, Sarah and Luke are starting to push each other around. Cara rushes to stop them before they get hurt, but Sarah's already on the floor crying. Cara lectures Luke. She's aware that he's getting more and more worked up, but she just can't seem to stop. Luke accuses Cara of always taking his sister's side and how unfair it all is.

Cara's phone rings and it's her husband, Tom. He's on his way home and just wants to check in. He hears the screaming in the background and makes a well-meaning, but ultimately triggering comment, "Just take away their iPad and play a game, they'll cool down. It always works for me."

Cara tries to distract them with the snacks she's prepared. But Luke isn't having it; his rant is now in full swing. Sarah's eating her cheese but taking the veggies out ... of her mouth ... after she's chewed them ... thoroughly. She's sitting by the sofa and tries stuffing the chewed-up veggies between the pillows. Cara would really like to calmly explain to Sarah that she shouldn't do that and ask her to clean up the mess she's made, but instead:

"Damn it, Sarah, that's disgusting! Why? Why would you do this? Look at the sofa!" She takes away her plate and throws it on the kitchen counter. Luke's still following her and lamenting over the unfairness of his sister's existence. Cara snaps and tells him to shut up and go to his room. She sees him tear up and shuffle up the stairs. Sarah looks at her, half smiling, half judging, and quickly hops upstairs too.

And so, in the much-desired, but also soul-gnawing quiet of the living room, amidst the spit-out vegetables, the torn-up paper, the sharp Lego edges waiting on her bare foot … Cara's spiral begins.

Why am I so short-tempered? Oh, look at this mess. They haven't even finished their snacks. Everyone's upset. We never seem to have any fun together anymore. Maybe they just want attention. Well, that seems quite reasonable, actually, and I am giving them attention. Maybe they want to irritate me so they can enjoy watching my huge reaction. They know what I want from them and how I expect them to behave. They should just do it. Why can't they just do one thing I ask with no fuss? Don't they love me?

Parenting is hard; not all the time, but much of the time. I read parenting books. I belong to Facebook groups. I look at Pinterest for parenting tips. I have read many, many books on parenting. I still lose my cool. I still react without thinking. When I get to my breaking point, beyond the level of frustration I can tolerate, I yell and threaten. I intimidate with punishments that I have no intention of following through with because I don't know what else to do. I am not proud. In fact, I am embarrassed afterward but I probably won't tell anyone what I did. I do these things because I don't know what to do differently. I consider myself an educated, resourceful, and driven parent. I want to do the right thing. I want to make my parenting decisions by blending science and facts with my gut instincts. I know who I am. But what am I missing?

Do these paragraphs ever represent your internal dialog? It is a common – one might say universal – experience to doubt our parenting skills and decisions. In other words, join the club. This book is here to validate how you feel, comfort you, and then push you to grow beyond your current level of thinking and comfort zone. As I do with all my clients, I will meet you where you are and describe the current state of parenting for many people. Next, I will share with you the smart and surefire means for achieving your parenting goals. Imagine this instead:

Cara is finishing an email to her boss when Luke comes into the room, clearly frustrated. He says, "Mommy, Sarah keeps touching my Legos even though I told her not to." Cara takes five deep breaths, hits save on the draft email, and gives Luke her full attention.

"Luke, it seems like you are frustrated right now. Do you want to tell me what happened?"

Immediately, she can see his shoulders drop and

relax and the tone of his voice softens. He begins to share his side of the story.

"Yes, Sarah came barging into the playroom. I was already playing and building with the Legos. She started taking them, didn't even ask me first, and then knocked over my tower. It's not fair. When I yelled at her, she didn't even care. You need to punish her and make her give back my Legos."

Cara replies, "It seems like you are feeling frustrated and mad because your sister did something that you think is unfair. She took your Legos and ruined what you were building. Is that right?"

"Yes, and she did it all without even asking me," Luke reinforces.

"And, she did it all without asking you, which is not polite, is it? I can see why you would feel frustrated and mad with her."

"You can?" Luke asks.

"Yes, I can," Cara replies. "I don't like to be treated unfairly either. I also feel mad and maybe even annoyed when someone takes my things without my permission."

"Yeah, it's just rude!" Luke emphasizes. "What are you going to do about it?"

"*WE* are going to sit down with Sarah and talk about your feelings, her actions, and how we could do things differently next time. How does that sound?" Cara asks.

"I like that plan, Mommy. Let's go," Luke says enthusiastically. Cara quickly finishes her email and then heads off to mediate the Lego situation.

It is possible to parent in ways that ensure both your and your children's needs are met. It is a relationship, after all, and relationships are give-and-take. Even very little people can learn to take responsibility for their role in each relationship. There are concepts and strategies that I can help you put into place that will resolve much (not all) of your parental guilt and support you to raise children who are healthy and happy while maintaining your sanity!

Parenting is hard but you are not alone. *We* can do hard things, not you, not I, *we*. I am here to support you through this process, so that you come out on the other side a parent who feels at peace with their decisions.

2

THE PATH TO PARENTAL PEACE OF MIND

"And, when you want something, all the universe conspires in helping you to achieve it."

— PAULO COELHO

When I first began teaching, I thought I had to have all the answers. I worked with children who were primarily nonverbal, severely developmentally delayed, and often displayed aggressive behaviors. I had fantastic mentors to support me. I was creative and hard-working. If I didn't know the answer, I would find it out, because that was my job. I was the expert. I wasted quite a few years putting this pressure on myself, but I was a very good teacher.

Two things happened that drastically changed how I viewed my role as a teacher and support person to my students' families. Every year, as I met my new students, there was always the little voice in my head asking, "Is this going to be the student you can't figure out? Is this going to be the one who shows everyone that you have no idea what you are doing, that you are a fraud?" Eventually, this did happen, at least from my perspective. I worked with a top-notch school team, psychologists, therapists, and administrators, who were student-centered, open-minded, and hardworking. This family was very willing to trust us and collaborate. Still, we could not figure out this kiddo. She was extremely aggressive toward peers and adults alike. I did not have the knowledge or skill set to change her behavior. I was not the expert anymore. I needed to learn a new way.

A year or so later, I attended a conference on supporting children with neurodiverse backgrounds. Presenters included doctors, neuroscientists, motor therapists, and psychiatrists. It was a three-day conference. At the mid-morning break on the first day, I went into the bathroom and cried because I was so overwhelmed by what I did not know. When I was done crying, I put on my big girl panties and decided I was going to learn and understand everything these people were offering. Ten years later, I earned my PhD in infant and early childhood development from that same group of people. Some of my key takeaways were:

- I am the expert on some things, not all things.
- The collaborative process with an open-minded team achieves the highest results.
- Best practices apply to teaching, parenting, and all human interactions.

These ideas translate into parenting very seamlessly. Of course, I want to be using best practices as a parent, too. I want to be doing what it takes so that my children are emotionally intelligent, have a strong moral compass, work hard, take risks, persist, and use all the resources available to them. I read articles, books, and websites, scouring them for the most up-to-date information on child-rearing. I asked my pediatrician many questions at each visit. Sometimes I found useful information. Sometimes I found contradictory information. Other times, I found ideas that did not at all jive with my intuition or values. I realized that I had to sort through a good deal of noise to find kernels of what would work for me and my family. It was a lot of work that led to self-doubt, anger, and guilt. As time went on, I realized that there are some core principles and practices that work every time, no matter the children's age or developmental level. In fact, these core ideas worked even as my children grew and went through more and more milestones. I was finally able to quickly get rid of what didn't work and choose to do what did work and felt right. However, I was not done learning.

As my children grew, it became very apparent that I was going to have to move outside of my comfort zones in order to best be able to advocate for them. I am not particularly comfortable with aggression or being assertive. However, there are times when my children needed me to experience those uncomfortable emotions to make sure they had what they needed. I had to confront a daycare provider who was not meeting my child's emotional needs. I had to have conversations with other important adults in my children's lives to ensure that my priorities toward my parenting goals were being supported. I also had to realize that I don't have to have all the answers. I have a support system. Many experienced, loving, and well-informed people in my life care for me. They validate how I am feeling; they listen without judgment; they offer advice when asked ... I am not in this alone. The emotional relief I felt when I realized that I did not have to have all the answers and that I had a support system who would lovingly and effectively champion me was a transformative moment.

I am not a perfect teacher or a perfect parent. However, when my daughters were roughly eleven and thirteen years old, I had a life-changing realization. There was no particular situation that prompted it, but one day I realized that my kids are good kids. As I continued to reflect, I was more specific. I thought to myself: *My girls have a moral compass. They have hobbies and ideas that they are passionate about. They have good work ethic. They have social justice issues that they are willing to fight for. And they are good friends.* All of this came together to bring me an overwhelming sense of peace. Do I think they are perfect? Of course not. Their grandparents certainly do, though. However, they have a strong emotional foundation that will support them to thrive, take risks, and weather life's challenges. Will they make mistakes? I hope so. I hope they make many, many mistakes. I hope they reflect on those mistakes and learn from them. That's the circle of a life well-lived, in my humble opinion.

Currently, I continue to work with parents of children who have vulnerabilities relating and communicating. I teach full-time and have a private practice. I decided to write this book because I have been sharing its contents in many forms for more than fifteen years. The fundamental ideas presented here apply to parenting, teaching, and pretty much all other human interactions.

I feel that it is important to use our time wisely. This book sorts through the noise and trends and goes right for the essentials of parenting. Additionally, the ideas presented here are foundational to all impactful human interactions, not just that of a parent and child. After attending one of my workshops, I have had people come back to me and say, “Hey, I used those techniques with my husband, my mother-in-law....” The concepts presented here get right to the human experience, hear it, validate it, and allow us to work together to move forward, whether the experience was comfortable or uncomfortable. In fact, I now *love* it when someone says, “I can’t do that. It’s hard.” The victory bells go off in my head as I think, “Challenge accepted.” And my reply is always, “It is hard and that’s okay, because we can do hard things." Then, we move forward together, as a team, to break down the problem and co-create a solution. There is almost nothing more satisfying than facing a dilemma head-on and creating a win-win resolution. This is my wish for you.

3

AMPLIFY YOUR PARENTING

"One can choose to go back toward safety or forward toward growth. Growth must be chosen again and again; fear must be overcome again and again."

— ABRAHAM MASLOW

When we first decide to become parents, we are immediately bombarded with information about how to be the *best* parent. During pregnancy, we research what to eat, how much to sleep, how to reduce stress, how to exercise. We are also given lots of unsolicited advice on these same topics. We want to be the best parents we can be but it's a lot of information to sort through. We learn to keep some of it and that other pieces of information don't fit into our way of thinking or our experiences. It can be difficult to decide what information is important at the time. We often become mentally and emotionally invested in a certain type of practice or a certain way of thinking only to realize that it isn't the right fit for us, that we've wasted time and resources when we could have been doing something differently or better. Throughout your life, you have been on many emotional and mental pendulums. In this book, I am going to teach you how to confidently get off that pendulum, knowing that you have the foundations to be a good parent and a good human.

First, we are going to dive into your child's internal world. As we better understand the what and the why behind their actions, we will then be able to make strategic parenting decisions. Understanding what is to be expected and what is typical at each developmental level will help you make reasonable expectations for yourself and your child. It also allows you to handle situations that don't go well with a level of grace as you expand your own understanding of what your child is experiencing and trying to accomplish as they grow through each stage in their life. You are going to have the language, the knowledge, and the skills to parent from a place without judgment.

Next, we are going to explore your internal experiences starting with your dreams for your child. From the instant that we know we're going to be parents; we start dreaming of what we would like our child's life to be like. We dream about what kind of person we want them to be, what values we want them to hold, the experiences we can provide for them. Most of us fluctuate as we're dreaming between the basics – being able to provide a safe home with food and love – to being able to send them to an Ivy League college and on to an amazing, seven-figure career. Our children will likely fall somewhere in the middle of that range. But these dreams will carry through with us as our children grow and go through each developmental milestone. Parents will have to adjust and adapt to our changing child and our changing world. This is okay; it's expected. It may be very hard at times, but we can do it. You are going to learn what you need to know about yourself to be able to ride the highs and lows of parenting.

Once we have explored your child's and your own inner emotional worlds, you will learn some very simple but highly impactful ways to interact with your child on a daily basis that will help you both to move toward those dreams you expressed. You can have playful, silly, and lovely interactions with your child that are specifically meant to support and expand their abilities to communicate, manage emotions, solve problems, and become their best selves, all while bringing you a sense of confidence and peace in your parenting decisions.

Finally, we will look realistically at what can and will go wrong. Roadblocks will occur. Embarrassing, frustrating, and hurtful things will happen. We know this. We will explore some of the things that we might be able to anticipate and how to respond to those that surprise us. Life will throw us curve balls and that is okay because we can do hard things. You will become comfortable with the idea that you do not have to have all the answers and your child does not, and should not, always do what you want them to do. This is how you get to peaceful parenting.

We break the steps down in this way:

- Amplify those Feelings (Chapter 4)
- Move and Power through the emotions (Chapter 5)
- Launch your wonder (Chapter 6)
- Interact with purpose (Chapter 7)

- Find your inner child (Chapter 8)
- Yield to the gray (Chapter 9)

Each chapter will begin with *Key Concepts* to help you focus on the most important ideas presented there and to familiarize you with the vocabulary. Next, there will be a theory section, that describes concepts relevant to the chapter topic. The theory section explains the why behind children's visible actions, typical developmental patterns and milestones, and the hierarchy of emotional foundations that we will build on. Finally, you will find a *Try It Now* section that gives you specific actions to try to help you integrate the information presented in the theory section. You will be able to see how the ideas relate to real life. There are many interpretations of the exercises. As you practice the activities, you may feel awkward. That is okay. Until you internalize the practices, you will need to keep attempting them and adjusting. Some very unexpected things may happen, and that is okay too. The chapters are best understood if you read them in order. The information from one chapter builds on the one before it. Take your time, have fun, learn, and grow, without the pressure of excellence.

We are not looking for perfection, but movement

toward more peaceful parenting practices. No one is a perfect parent. However, in this book, you will learn how to parent with intent, playfulness, empathy, and grace in ways that help you fulfill your dreams to be a good parent.

4

AMPLIFY THOSE FEELINGS

"The best and most beautiful things in the world cannot be seen or even touched. They must be felt with the heart."

— HELEN KELLER

Key Concepts:

- Emotional profile
- "I Feel" statements
- Notice and wonder
- Neutral language

When we take our children to the pediatrician for a well visit, we are often given a list of what they can be expected to do at their age. These checklists usually focus on motor skills such as rolling over, crawling, walking, and jumping, and communication skills like babbling and talking. The focus tends to be on what the children can do. There is a huge piece missing from this conversation, though. We are not taught what their inner emotional experiences are like and how those evolve as our kids grow and learn. Sure, we notice when they are angry or happy and we respond to that. However, we are not explicitly taught to pay attention to our children's emotions as a developmental element. They have feelings, – we know this. They express their feelings in a variety of ways. We notice them and then react to them. Is there more to it than that? Yes, there definitely is.

EMOTIONAL PROFILES

When humans are infants, they only need to express a few emotions to help them get what they need. They show happiness to express contentment and joy. They show upset when they are hungry or need a diaper change. They use curiosity to help them explore their world, typically starting with their own hands and feet. So, they are safe, growing, and learning. Their emotional profile may simply be:

- Happy
- Sad
- Fear
- Curiosity
- Disgust
- Anger

Although, a teenage boy once asked me in all sincerity, "How many emotions do girls have? I'm pretty sure I only have two." I assured him he definitely had more than two.

As they grow, children have more experiences and their emotions become more complex. Their emotional range grows. Eventually, they will need more complex words to accurately describe those internal experiences. Their emotional profile may include these feelings and more:

Feelings Wheel

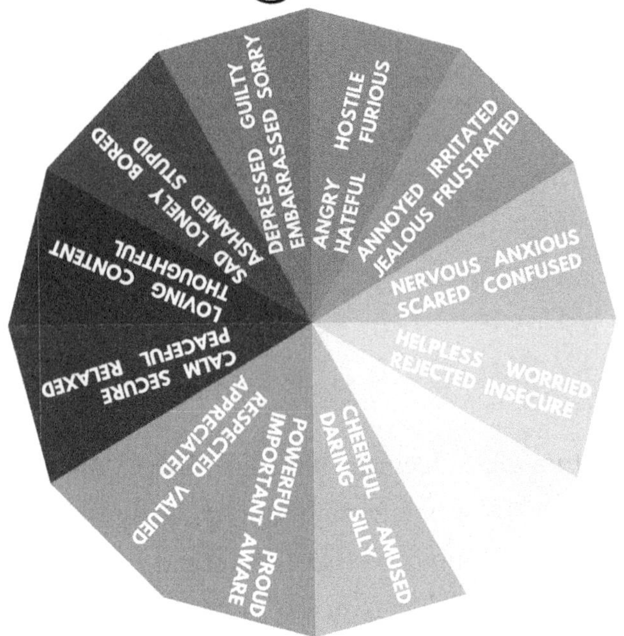

They will want more accurate words to represent their internal experiences. This is true for our children and for us.

Why do we experience emotions in the first place? What purpose do they serve? Quite simply, emotions are a source of information for our brains, very much like the five senses. We don't, on a conscious level, often think about all of the information that is coming into our brains from our five senses. We trust our brains to be using this information as they see fit. This is the same with our emotions. Unless you are brought up to pay very specific attention to your emotions, you don't tend to think about them, label them, or consider what their purpose is until they become really intense and force you to act on them. Most of the time our emotions are doing their job. They are not positive or negative. They are simply informing our brain about how we are responding to our environment.

Emotions give information to our brain to help it make the best decisions that it can. It is our brain's job to integrate information that is coming from outside of the body – via our five senses – with information from inside our body, like emotions and memories. We want to help our children integrate these ideas in the most successful way. Helping them to understand what is physically happening in their body when they experience certain emotions supports them to consider the physical and the emotional at the same time. We want to do this so that eventually they can self-identify what they are feeling. However, we want them to do that accurately. Identifying emotions mistakenly may lead us to choose an unsuccessful way to handle them.

I had a student who was very upset with me one day because I dismissed the class late for lunch. He pounded his fist on the desk and he said very loudly, "I feel depressed because you made us leave late for lunch!" I was very proud of him for using "I feel" statements and telling me with his words what emotion he thought he was experiencing. However, he needed some additional information in that moment. So, I let him know that feeling depressed usually means feeling sad for many days, weeks, and even months in a row. Then I asked him if he thought he was feeling depressed. He was open-minded and willing to change his thinking. He said that he was probably feeling angry or frustrated. The way we would support someone who is feeling depressed is very different from the way that we would support someone who's feeling a very short-term level of frustration. This is why accurately labeling emotions is important. So, how do we get there?

The process we want to eventually teach our children looks like this:

- Notice what is happening inside your body, i.e., physical cues;
- Wonder about what that emotion might be;
- Label that emotion accurately.

As parents, we will have certain responsibilities at each step in this process.

NOTICE AND WONDER

Our bodies give us clues about what feeling state we are experiencing. We don't always notice it until the emotion is really intense. For example, when my muscles are tight and my skin is red and hot, I might be feeling mad, angry, frustrated, embarrassed, or humiliated. If I have a lump in my throat, my chest feels heavy, and I feel the need to lower my eyes, I may be sad, disappointed, lonely, or hurt. If I have a fluttering in my stomach, my skin is sweating, and my muscles are tight, I may feel excited, nervous, thrilled, or terrified. Children need to know that this happens inside their bodies and learn to notice it. This takes practice and reflection. The reflective process typically takes place after the child was feeling a big emotion. We don't want to do this until they are calm and can reasonably "hear" what we are saying. This is where the "I notice" statements come in. We are giving them information that they probably were not aware of. For example, "I noticed that your face was getting red, your eyes were squinted, and your muscles were tight." Now, the "I wonder" statement, "I wonder if you were feeling mad because you could not get a toy when we were in the store." We tell them what we noticed and then explain what it led us to think; we point out the cause and effect.

We do not want to tell people how they are feeling. I'm not sure if anyone has ever tried to tell you how you are feeling, but we typically don't like it. Even from someone who is well-meaning, it can come across as presumptuous and arrogant. We want to wonder aloud with our child and put the idea out there in the middle of us, so we can talk about it and examine it together. We are creating a situation where we can collaborate to increase our child's self-awareness. We are giving them information that they probably weren't aware of, helping them to determine if this is in fact how they were feeling, and then together we can decide what to do about it when it happens again. It will happen again. Learning to be reflective often happens first through

20/ 20 hindsight until we are better able to process our emotions in the moment. So, the process includes thinking about how I felt in the past, comparing to how I am feeling now, and then how I may feel in the future under similar circumstances.

One very simple way to get into the practice of reflecting on our emotions is to take time noticing and wondering how you feel. I was well into adulthood before I realized on a conscious level that my neck gets red and hot when I am angry. It creeps up into my face and there is nothing I can do about it. But now that I know that happens, I am much faster at being able to respond to that emotion and to deal with it in appropriate ways. Simply using "I feel" statements can be a very powerful way to practice identifying how you feel. Eventually, you will add more complexity to that process. You may add a "what" and a "why" to associate with the emotion. For example, "I am sad when I yell at the kids because I feel like I have failed them and myself." Notice what physical things are happening inside your body at the same time. Do you have a lump in your throat? Is your heart racing? Are your muscles tense and tight? These are the first indicators that you are feeling a certain type of emotion. There are many common ways that humans physically experience the same emotions – for example, a racing heartbeat when we're excited or nervous. However, these will also be individual to you. Get comfortable with this practice because it is a very powerful thing to be able to teach your children.

Teach your children how to *notice* and *wonder*. The notice-and-wonder process takes judgment out of the situation. When we judge how our children are behaving, it usually means we are making assumptions and coming to a conclusion, which may or may not be accurate, about their actions. Children become defensive when they feel they are being judged, particularly if we are incorrect in our assumptions. When we feel defensive, we are likely to shut down or become angry, neither of which is a mindset for solving a problem. The notice and wonder process allows us to put a particular situation into neutral terms. It is much easier for us to talk about the things that make us feel uncomfortable and vulnerable when we can use neutral language. When talking to a child, I might say, "I noticed your face is red and your voice is getting loud. I wonder if you are feeling mad." Simply explaining what you notice helps raise the child's awareness about those things. That is a much different conversation then if I made a judgmental statement like, "Stop yelling just because you are mad." It is the same information but delivered in a very different way. The child is hearing, "It is not okay for me to be mad," and that their feelings are not valid. Noticing and the wondering allow us to have a collaboration about the child's feelings. We are able to put these ideas in the middle and talk about them. In this way, we can constructively get to the root of the problem and talk about what to do next.

It is helpful to note that using "why" questions with children will not be effective until they get a little bit older and have some self-reflective capacities. Asking them why they did something may backfire and lead to a defensive response from the child. They may have no idea why they did something, or they may not have the vocabulary to explain what they were thinking and feeling. As a general rule, when you notice children asking "Why" questions, then you can begin using them, as well. For typically developing children, this is usually between forty-two and forty-nine months old.

When my youngest daughter was about seven years old, she saw me working on my laptop. There was a small pebble or something underneath the "m" key. So, I had popped the key off to get the object out from underneath it. I left the room and came back a few minutes later to find the "m" key was gone. I asked my daughter if she knew where it went, and she said yes. She had taken it outside and buried it in the yard. Of course, I asked her why she did this. She had no idea why she did it. So, to this day, I chalk it up to curiosity.

While I recommend using "why" questions sparingly with younger children, it is useful in helping older children practice communicating and articulating their feelings and ideas. Again, you can follow their lead to know when this is appropriate to incorporate into your interaction style. When they begin to ask why questions, then you know that it is an appropriate time to start integrating them into your dialog. Why questions are particularly useful as we help kids delve deeply into their curiosities. Consider this conversation around a painting activity:

Sally: "Can I have more paint and shaving cream?"

Mom: "Why do you want more paint and shaving cream?"

Sally: "Because I am excited to keep mixing yellow and blue together to see if it makes green."

Why questions can be used to help children articulate their thinking, consider cause and effect relationships, and begin self-reflective practices. Initially, we may need to support them with some of the words they need to accurately express themselves. Always remember in these moments to praise their fabulous ideas, so they continue to want to explore and ask more whys.

NEUTRAL LANGUAGE

One exercise that may help you to become just a little more open-minded and flexible is to try taking the word *should* out of your thinking. When things *should* be a certain way or my children *should* behave in a certain way or they *should* think and feel a certain way, that's a predetermination that can lead us to being stuck. If I'm willing to use *could* instead of should that opens up many more possibilities on how a certain situation might unfold. For example, my child *should* be able to sit at the table and complete their homework by themselves. If this is my assumption, and then it is not the reality, there will be tension when this is not the result. Compare that to, my child *could* complete their homework fairly independently if I set a visual timer and check in with them three times to counterbalance any frustration or anxiety they may be feeling. *Black and White*: They *should* be able to complete their homework by themselves. *Gray and nuanced*: They *could* complete their homework with some flexible supports and emotional check-ins. Try consciously taking the word *should* out of the language you use and see how much more flexible your thinking becomes. *Should* tends to convey judgment, where *could* conveys possibilities. We want to take judgment out of the equation. This book is meant to give you neutral language and frameworks for understanding and communicating about your child's (and your own) emotional profiles. Maya Angelou said, "Do the best you can until you know better. Then when you know better, do better." Don't judge yourself on how you react to your children. You *should* not parent a certain way. Learning to be kind to yourself, reflect, and grow helps you to then do the same for your child.

Whatever your children's emotional profile looks like; it is okay. They are entitled to feel what they feel. All emotions are valid. They have a purpose and a meaning. They are not right or wrong. They are not positive or negative. They may make us feel comfortable or uncomfortable, and that is okay too. For example, we tend to think of anger and fear as negative emotions and conversely, joy and pride as positive emotions. The truth is, they are simply comfortable or uncomfortable. Either way, they are giving our brains information, and we have to decide what to do with that information. Your child may feel angry because a sibling took something without asking for permission, rightly so. We feel unjust and angry when people take what is not theirs. This reaction is reasonable, expected, and valid. We have all felt that way at one time or another. We do not want to tell our children *not* to feel that way. They are entitled to feel that way. What we have to help them do is notice the physical signs, choose the correct words to represent that experience, and ultimately, we want our children to be able to effectively handle whatever the world throws at them. Being able to regulate a wide range of emotions will help them to adapt and successfully make their way through life.

TRY IT NOW

Exercise 1 – Record It!

A helpful and quite sweet exercise to help build your ability to identify your child's emotions is to video record them while they are playing or interacting with others. Go back and watch the video without sound. Take your time and focus on body language, eye gaze, facial expressions, and actions. This will help you to actively wonder what the child is thinking and feeling. Notice if you can follow the child's train of emotions and thoughts. By all means, hop into the play afterward and find out if you were correct.

Exercise 2 – Turn Should into Could!

For the next two weeks, take the word "should" out of your vocabulary. You can replace it with "could," some other word, or remove it altogether. Notice how removing this word changes your perspective. What assumptions are you forced to confront? How does this open you to alternative ways of thinking and behaving, to more flexible views of why your children behave the way they do? This activity will help you consciously consider your black and white thinking and help you to consider some possible gray areas instead.

5

MOVE AND POWER THROUGH THE EMOTIONS

"Your emotions make you human. Even the unpleasant ones have a purpose. Don't lock them away. If you ignore them, they just get louder and angrier."

— SABAA TAHIR

Key Concepts:

- Emotional world
- Regulation, co-Regulation, self-Regulation
- Mirroring/ counterbalancing
- Affective attunement

"Your dreams are my dreams." Dr. Gil Tippy says this upon first meeting and working with parents. He has coached thousands of families and their support systems to understand children in a holistic and empathetic framework. We all have dreams for our children, and we want them validated. When we seek help to become better parents, we want to know that our ideas are important, that what we want for our children is still the main goal. We just need some help to get there while keeping our sanity intact.

Take a few minutes now and write down your dreams for your children. They can be short-term, long-term, simple, or complex. There are no right or wrong answers. Keep them handy throughout this chapter.

When children are young, we begin the process of setting them up for success. We may enroll them in music classes, art classes, sports, playgroups, all the things that we believe will help them to develop into happy, healthy, well-adjusted adults. We want to provide them with a variety of experiences so that they can learn and grow. We also realize – as they begin to turn into their own person – that we may have to adjust to and adapt the dreams that we started with when our children were small. There was no way, for example, that my oldest daughter was going to be a soccer star. She and her friend would stand in front of the goal holding hands, talking to each other, pretty much oblivious to what else was taking place on the field. That is okay, she has many other strengths. Some families experience more serious complications such as a learning disability, social anxiety, or family stressors that dramatically change their situation. We still have dreams for our children, even under stressful and traumatic circumstances. But as the years go on, we change and adapt them. So that is what we need to teach our children to do, to be flexible and adaptable. We do that by supporting their ability to experience and regulate a range of emotions.

REGULATION AND CO-REGULATION

Children will and do need to experience a range of emotions. It is our job, as parents, to help them realize what they are feeling, give it a name, notice what is happening inside their body at the time, and then decide what to do about it. The more feelings a person can experience and tolerate, the more flexible and adaptable they will be.

As parents, we support our children to manage or regulate their range of emotions. By regulation, I mean the ability to experience and tolerate certain degrees and intensities of a particular emotion. We all have a range within which we can tolerate certain emotions. You may be able to tolerate a large degree of anger but very little sadness. You may be able to regulate – i.e., experience and manage within socially acceptable terms – intense feelings of excitement but only small amounts of aggression. We can all create a profile of ourselves considering each emotion and our ability to tolerate and manage it. The same is true for our children. This is one of the pieces missing from the pediatrician's wellness forms mentioned in Chapter 4. Yet, we must be consciously thinking about how well our children can regulate emotions, which ones are easier, which ones are more difficult, and why. For our children to be well-adjusted and emotionally healthy, they need to be able to regulate a wide range of emotions throughout their lives. When we can manage a wide range of emotions, we are adaptable and flexible, and thereby, generally more successful in more situations.

When the regulation comes from another person, this is called *co-regulation*. The parent or caregiver is providing support for the child to tolerate, work through, and manage their emotions. We may use a soothing tone, rub their back, swaddle or hug them to assist them through this. Eventually, we teach them to regulate and manage their emotions somewhat on their own. As they get older, children can begin to learn to self-regulate. Eventually, our caregiver co-regulating role becomes smaller, and the child can self-regulate more independently. That is the ultimate goal for all humans – to be able to regulate most of our emotions by ourselves. We will never be able to regulate them all on our own and that is okay. We are social creatures for a reason.

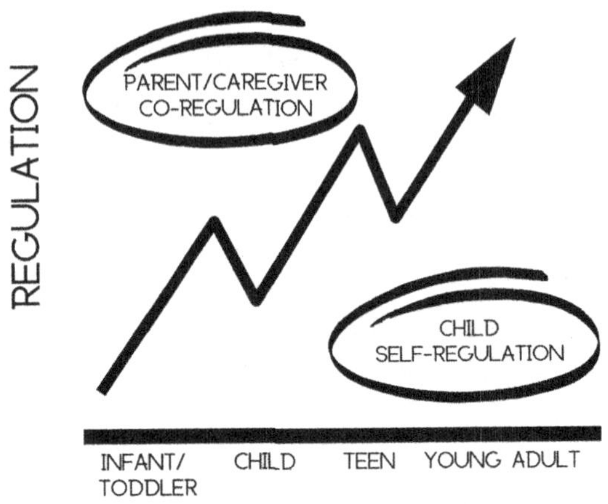

To be able to effectively co-regulate, we must first be aware of our own emotional state. It is nearly impossible to think about the emotional profile of our children without also reflecting on our own patterns. We may begin to ask ourselves questions about why our children behave in certain ways. Why do they avoid certain things or why are they attracted to certain things? We may notice that our children love excitement, leaping from the highest places, trying new experiences without a second thought, or jumping into a new friendship. They seem to seek thrills, stimulation, and satisfaction from intense situations. Conversely, we may notice that they avoid staying in any kind of sad emotion. Instead, they may distract themselves, change the subject, or completely circumvent any conversation around that emotion. It is our job to notice and wonder about these patterns. What developmental or emotional need is being met through the exciting events? Why does my child avoid feeling sad?

An important piece to include in our emotional conversations is to ask ourselves questions about our internal experiences. Simply asking, "How am I feeling right now?" can be a vital question and should influence how we decide to respond to any situation. If I am feeling angry right now, I may not the best person to co-regulate with my upset child. Consider Cara's story at the beginning of Chapter 1. She has been helping Luke with his math assignment. "It's addition, just use your fingers to count," Cara says.

"That's not how my teacher does it," Luke argues.

"She said we have to use the 'Ten Frame' and counters to show our work."

"What is a 'Ten Frame?' You have ten fingers, right, isn't that the same thing?" Cara is confused and frustrated. She thinks, "He is adding numbers up to ten. This is not difficult. Why does the teacher need to make it difficult? This is not how I learned math. It's ridiculous and makes the whole online learning even harder than it already is!"

"No, Mom, it's not the same thing. I have to do it the way the teacher told us," Luke insists. Cara decides to walk away, take some deep breaths, and splash water on her face. She enters the bathroom to find that Sarah has created a 'witches brew' in the sink with the soap, shampoo, conditioner, hand lotion, and just about every other liquid she could reach. It's a huge mess. Cara is already frustrated and close to her breaking point.

Logically, Cara thinks, "I know this is what she is expected to do at this age. She is supposed to experiment with textures, gravity, chemistry, whatever. But I will have to be the one to clean this up (if I want it done right!). I just can't deal with this right now!" As she is taking stock of her emotions in the situation and their intensity, she may want to tag out in this moment. If she is angry, frustrated, and close to her breaking point, she is probably not going to respond to Sarah's actions with calm and curiosity. It is okay to ask for help and have another adult move in to help. Maybe you are the only adult there, so you need to use a few of your own strategies to drain off your emotions before you proceed. Knowing ourselves is vital to successful parenting.

Adults need to understand what their overall emotional profile looks like. What emotions are you comfortable experiencing? What emotions do you avoid? What is your tolerance level for each of these emotions? Perhaps, you can tolerate lots of frustration but only a little bit of jealousy. Maybe you have a very short fuse when you feel something is unfair but can endure a good degree of anxiety. Adult profiles will be as individual as the children's. In order to better understand what our emotional profiles look like, it is helpful to practice self-reflective activities that specifically help us explore our emotional range and tolerance. As we understand this in ourselves, we can more clearly appreciate what is happening in our children's emotional worlds.

Truly being self-reflective means being able to hold the past, the present, and the future in our minds all at the same time. When we notice how we are feeling in the moment (present), can accurately identify why we are feeling this way (past), we can then decide how to respond and what to do about the same emotion the next time we experience it (future). It is not an easy task, but it is achievable and important in helping us to improve our ability to co-regulate and self-regulate. The pause that is created in the reflective process between *noticing* how you feel and then *deciding* how to respond to that emotion (rather than reacting to it) is a huge developmental milestone and the key to opening up our children's ability to take on the reflective process for themselves. We model and explain the process to them – co-regulation – and then teach them how to do it on their own – self-regulation. It takes many, many tries, examples, mistakes, and lots of grace before we or our children will be proficient with the reflective process, but it is a skill that will support them to be able to handle more emotions with greater intensities throughout their lifetimes.

COUNTERBALANCING AND MIRRORING

Let's go back and think about children's early life and how development occurs within the brain. The human brain's job is to look for patterns in the world. It wants to be as efficient as possible. It does not want to have to learn the same things every day. When it notices patterns, those parts of the brain that are involved in that experience will wire together, remembering what happened, so it can repeat the process or recall the information much faster the next time. John Ratey coined the phrase, "Neurons that fire together, wire together." A baby may realize when he smiles at mommy, mommy smiles back. Tomorrow he remembers and smiles at mommy so that she will smile in return. As the brain continues to notice more patterns, memories are made and the brain begins to create context. The context helps all future experiences to be more efficient, deeper, and richer. This is also true for emotional understanding. When we notice emotional patterns, we use them as our anchors and our jumping-off points for future emotional experiences.

As parents, it is important for us to be in tune with our children's emotional states. In Chapter 4, we discussed identifying emotions. When parents can accurately identify how a child is feeling and why, we are attuned to their feelings or their affect. We do this through our actions, our tone of voice, proximity, facial expressions, and word choice. We often respond to emotions without even realizing it is what we are doing. Have you ever noticed when you see a little person that is upset you tend to get down at their eye level and use a soft comforting tone of voice? You are using nonverbal communication to convey empathy. In a very brief moment, your brain identified how that child was feeling and made the decision to counterbalance it by soothing and co-regulating. Almost instantaneously, you realized how the child was feeling and what you needed to do. When they are feeling intense emotions – particularly those that they have a hard time regulating by themselves – we know that we need to act to reduce the intensity of that emotion; in other words, we have to counterbalance it. We may take actions to comfort our children and reduce their emotions. We may also join the interaction with a complementary emotion in order to reduce the intensity of the emotion.

Consider when a child is feeling angry, we may try to soothe them by validating how they are feeling, thereby reducing the intensity of their anger. We may also bring an opposite emotion to the situation in order to help reduce the child's intensity. When the child is angry, we may join the situation conveying a sense of peace, not in a way that diminishes the validity of the child's emotions, but in a way that conveys another emotional option. We work in that moment, to bring them toward our emotional state. We may say, "I can see that you are very angry. I understand why you feel this way. Do you want to talk about it?" Our body language in this instance will be open and neutral. We may put ourselves in an inferior position to the child, below their eye level for example, so that they can feel some sense of power. If the child is pacing out of anxiousness or anger, we may pull up two chairs and sit in one, creating an open invitation for the child to sit in the other. We are communicating that we are here to listen and support them. The nonverbal cues we give in this moment are just as important as the words we choose. Our total communication is meant to support the child in a way that reduces the intensity of the emotion that they are feeling.

Sometimes we may mirror the child when we are in a similar situation. We may mirror their body language and use the words that they are using in our conversation. Mirroring conveys empathy and joining. It says to the child that you recognize and validate their current emotional state. If a child is happy and bouncing up and down, we may also bounce up and down and mirror their facial expressions. Without saying a word, we are conveying that we understand how they feel, and we want to join them in this moment. Be cautious when using mirroring with intense emotions. Our purpose is always to validate but we do not want to escalate the situation and inadvertently increase an uncomfortable emotion. This may feel awkward at first. However, once you feel the attunement and emotional connection with your child, you will realize the power of mirroring and counterbalancing.

When we are affectively attuned with our children, it helps them to be more regulated and encourages them to communicate openly and freely. Go back to that list of dreams that you have for your children. What emotional profile do they need to possess and feel comfortable with to achieve those goals? For example, if you said you want your child to be an entrepreneur, they would need to be comfortable taking risks and with the feelings that come with making mistakes. If you want your child to understand the power of service and volunteering, they will need to express empathy and be able to tolerate the uncomfortable feelings of seeing people struggle. Stanley Greenspan said, "Adaptability is the highest form of human development." That idea is a foundation for my parenting decisions. It leads me to ask myself, "Am I supporting my children to be able to adapt, change course, rethink a situation when things do not go the way they planned?" My oldest daughter said to me once out of nowhere – I think she was about eleven years old at the time – "Our family motto is to 'Suck it up,' isn't it?" Well, we don't have that stitched on a pillow anywhere. However, I do expect my children to be self-aware, to notice what is happening inside their bodies, to accurately label their emotions, to know what resources are available to them, and to use those resources with a flexible mind. So, if that's what "Suck It Up" means, then yes.

Adaptability comes when we are confident that we can tolerate a wide range of emotions and intensity levels. If we can do that, then we can handle almost any situation that comes our way. These are levels of awareness and skills that we can teach our children, a little bit, at each step in their development. Dream big for yourself and your children. We can accomplish almost anything when we consciously evaluate the emotions we are experiencing, how they impact us, and what, if anything, we can do about it. I love to tell my kids, "If plan A doesn't work, that is okay, because there are twenty-five more letters in the alphabet." If plan Z doesn't work, we just move on to plan 1A. There are infinite possibilities. The only time we are not adaptable is when we give up.

"This seems like a college-level psychology class!" You definitely will need to practice the techniques shared in this chapter, especially if it is not how you were raised or trained. That's okay. You will make mistakes. That's okay, too. This is not about perfect parenting. It is about taking steps to be a better parent, through self-reflection and co-regulation. Believe it or not, children can begin to appreciate these concepts as soon as they can understand abstract ideas. When they realize that if the dog leaves the room, he still exists, they are conceptualizing abstract or symbolic ideas. I don't have to be able to touch the dog to know that it exists. I don't have to be able to hold "mad" to know that it is a real thing. Children can do this as early as eighteen to thirty months old. Of course, their language skills will also be a factor in how well they can receive and express the information. That being said, do not wait to begin including these types of interactions with your child. Be cautious and kind about your expectations for their understanding but give it a try. Even if your children are teens or adults, it is never too late. Feeling understood is a core human need. By being willing to discuss someone's emotions, you convey to them that you care about how they feel and want to be a part of that experience with them.

TRY IT NOW

Try mirroring and counterbalancing at least three times each. You will first need to consciously identify how the child is feeling and then decide, "Do I want to join this emotion or counterbalance it?" It is easier to begin with comfortable emotions while you are first learning how to integrate these strategies into your parenting. Remember, it may feel unnatural and awkward at first, but when you feel the connection you create, you will internalize the strategy for good.

6

LAUNCH YOUR WONDER

"Wherever you are, be there totally."

— ECKHART TOLLE

Key Concepts:

- Assumptions
- The Purpose of emotions
- Strengths-based approach
- Rupture and repair

ASSUMPTIONS

In Chapters 4 and 5, I discussed the importance of reflecting on our emotions and being able to accurately notice, label, and regulate them. Another important piece of the reflection process is beginning to consciously consider the assumptions that we are making in any given situation.

As a parent and teacher, I have often heard the phrase, "He/ she is just doing that to get attention." I absolutely hate that phrase. I've been very fortunate to work with some outstanding psychologists during my career. One of the first psychologists I ever worked with said this very simple but very powerful phrase that I have always remembered: All behavior has meaning. Everything we do as humans has a purpose. It is usually a means for us to try to have a need met. So that phrase, "He's just doing that to get attention," is completely dismissing the need that underlies the behavior.

It is our job as parents to figure out that need and then to help our children get that need met in a way that we can all live with. One shift in thinking that has helped me along this path is to assume intentionality. When we assume that a child is behaving in a specific way for a specific reason, we can remove judgment from our interaction. For example, if a child behaves in a way that seems provocative, perhaps purposely annoying his little sister until she is angry, rather than assume that he is "just doing it to get attention" or "just doing it to be mean," let's consider the developmental need his actions are fulfilling.

We all need to feel powerful, like we have control over at least some parts of our lives. Perhaps this is his way of exerting power. If so, this is a typical need for children. Instead of assuming that he is "just" doing it for a negative reason, we assume he is doing it with intentionality to meet a typical developmental need – the feeling of power. If we are correct, we can create opportunities for him to exert power in ways that we find acceptable rather than bugging little sister. Perhaps he gets to make choices on movie night, what movie we watch, what snack we eat. Perhaps he is allowed to create a magical world with blocks, and we allow him to lead the story narrative while we play secondary characters. In either scenario, it is a win-win-win. The child gets to experience power, his little sister is not annoyed, and we feel good about how we are supporting typical development in our children.

There are many ways to meet the need for feeling powerful – or any other emotion, for that matter. We have to be aware of the assumptions we are making before we decide how to proceed with our parenting choices. Again, this allows us to move forward using neutral language and nonjudgmental thinking in order to help our children grow into self-aware and emotionally intelligent people.

PURPOSE OF EMOTIONS

One way to frame our thinking within a neutral framework is to consider that all emotions have a job to do. The Disney movie *Inside Out* represents this idea beautifully for adults and children. Each of the five main emotional characters has a very specific and concrete role in the life of the little girl whose brain they live in. Let's explore some of the basic emotions together.

When teaching children specifically about emotions, I often start with disgust. It seems to be quite an easy concept to understand. I will often give them this example: You live in a "hunter and gatherer" community, and you are out in the woods looking for food. You come across a big, brown, steaming pile of something. It looks bad; it smells bad. And then I ask them would you eat it? Of course, they say no because they have figured out that I am talking about animal poop. They can very quickly understand that looking and smelling poop creates the feeling of disgust.

Next, we bring the idea to modern times. Say you are hungry and looking in the fridge for a snack. You reach way into the back and find a container that's been there for two months. You open it, there are furry, watery, smelly things on the top of whatever was originally in the container. Again, do you put a big spoon in there and take a bite of this? Of course, they always say, “No, that's disgusting.” So, it doesn't take long from there for children to realize that the purpose of disgust is to keep us healthy. We get the feeling of disgust when we are looking, touching, or smelling something that, if we consumed it, may make us sick. This jumping-off point for children really conceptualizes for them that each emotion has a particular job to do.

Typically, after that, we discuss fear. I usually start with a very extreme example like: If a bear was chasing you, how would you feel? They can easily give me some word that would be under the umbrella of fear or scared. Then we talk about what their brain would tell their body to do. It's usually one-step thinking for them to explain that their brain would tell their body to get out of that dangerous situation. So, children are generally able to understand the idea that the fundamental purpose of fear is to keep us safe. Does fear ever get in the way of something we may be attempting to do? Yes. We will discuss that in a little bit.

One of my absolutely favorite emotions to talk about with children is pride. Pride reinforces the choices that we have made. When we feel proud, it tells us that the action steps we took in order to achieve our goal were successful. It tells us that we put forth the appropriate effort, that we made effective decisions, and if we want to achieve that same goal or a similar goal again in the future, we already know the steps to take. This can be such a powerful tool for children.

When they understand what pride is communicating to them, children get a sense of agency and control over what happens to them. When children believe that they have the power to act and get the results that they want, there is a huge positive downstream effect. They become more confident. They are more likely to take calculated risks and create bigger goals for themselves. They are more likely to develop empathy because they know what it takes to be successful. Mistakes become less significant. When we help children to reflect on feeling proud and what brought them to that place, they are able to consciously decide to take those same successful actions again in the future.

One of the future conversations we may have with our children is the difference between pride and arrogance. As they get older, we want to keep the emotional conversations going to bring their awareness to the nuances of emotions. However, on a basic level, we want them to understand that emotions have a job to do.

Another emotion that I love talking with children about is curiosity. Curiosity leads us to explore our environment. It inspires us to create, to innovate, to understand the things that we are passionate about from the top to the bottom and from the inside out. Humans are naturally born curious. Exploring our environment is the way our brain begins to find those patterns that help it to be more efficient. Curiosity tends to be joyful, fun, and exciting. I often challenge children to create a phrase for curiosity to replace "Curiosity killed the cat." I want them to view curiosity as an emotion that leads to positive actions, learning, and growth. In many ways, curiosity is the counterbalance to some of the more extreme uncomfortable emotions like depression and hopelessness. When we are curious about our world, ourselves, and others, our brains are working to find out more. We are engaged and full of wonder. We are actively interacting with our world in ways that lead to an increase in comfortable emotions such as satisfaction, power, creativity, and value.

Consider a child who wants to dig a hole as deep as they can to see what is there, perhaps working toward reaching the other side of the planet. In the process, they will come in contact with many types of creatures to wonder about and explore. They will need to problem-solve when they encounter rocks too big to move. They will begin to think symbolically about what lies deeper that they cannot yet see. Their curiosity leads to action after action that creates a powerful flow of thinking, creating, and problem-solving. Humans are born curious so that we will explore and learn about our world. As parents, acknowledging this inherent trait and facilitating it, helps us to be aware of and perhaps create situations where our children can explore their curiosity. Science and innovation are two byproducts of this emotion.

Joy and sadness are two sides of the same coin.

They both help us to feel connected to other people and they remind us about what is important. Consider a family pet. It brings us great joy as we play with it and love it. We feel a bond with the pet and our family members who also love the pet the way we do. It becomes an important part of our lives. When it passes away, we feel sadness because it was so important to us. We also feel connected to our family members because we can empathize with how they feel. We know they feel sadness for the same reason we do. In this way, joy and sadness make us feel connected to others and remind us of what is important in life.

Anger is a significant concept to discuss with children. It is often described as a secondary emotion, meaning that there is typically another emotion underneath the anger. On a very basic level, it's helpful for children to understand that the purpose of anger is to inspire us to take action to solve a problem. I often use the example, "If you were on the playground and someone pushed you off the swing, how would you feel?" Children will easily answer "mad." We then continue talking about why it would make them mad and what they could do about it, so that the same situation or problem, does not happen again. There are many real-life examples to use when discussing anger. The conversations will be had again and again as children grow older and understand more about the world and justice. Anger can be very personal but there are also historical examples that can help children understand how we can use anger to solve social problems. We often feel angry when we think something isn't fair or is unjust. Taking action to solve that problem often will lessen our anger, give us a sense of agency, and can shift to feeling proud if we have successfully solved the problem. Many children are taught that anger is bad and they shouldn't feel that way. Rather, we must teach them that it has a purpose and how we respond to the emotion is what is most important.

There is no particular order in which it is appropriate to discuss the purpose of emotions. I would recommend using real-life, personal examples in your conversations. It is also a good time to reinforce that emotions are neither positive nor negative. Some make us feel comfortable, some make us feel uncomfortable, and that's okay. That is true now and it will be true if you live to be 110 years old. What is important is to be able to have that neutral conversation about what an emotion is telling me and what I am going to do about it.

Eventually, we will want to let children know that they can decide how they respond to their emotions. They may decide that they want to override certain emotions if they are in conflict with their goals. Let's go back to disgust. I know that its job is to make sure that I stay healthy. However, at some point, I need to decide if I'm going to listen to disgust or if I am going to veto it. Personally, I hated mushrooms through most of my adult life. I was in my mid-thirties when I discovered that mushrooms could be delicious. So, you can think about individuals having very personal and tailored interactions with each emotion and how they decide to respond to it. We know that the job of fear is to keep us safe. However, what if fear prevents me from auditioning for an acapella group that I want to join or from trying out for a sports team that I'm interested in? In those situations, fear is not keeping us safe. Fear is interfering with our future success. This example reinforces the idea that we must be consciously aware of what emotion we are experiencing so that we can decide how we want to respond to it. Do I want to listen to what it's telling me, or do I need to make a different decision based on what is best for me and my goals?

STRENGTHS-BASED APPROACH

As we continue to talk about children's emotional profiles, it is helpful if we not only use neutral language to remove judgment, but also view our child from a strengths-based perspective. Understanding what my child is good at: What are her natural inborn talents? What skills has she cultivated through hard work? This connects to emotional self-awareness because we also want to consider what emotional range is she comfortable with. Specifically, what emotions is she comfortable experiencing and what does she avoid? I'm going to use this information to help her in times when she is vulnerable.

If my child is full of curiosity and loves to explore but also has trouble tolerating the embarrassment of making mistakes, how can I strategically use her strengths to support areas of vulnerability? I may encourage her to play scientist and be her lab assistant who makes lots of mistakes. As the lab assistant who makes mistakes, I can use emotional narrative in my play, I may say things like "Oh boy, that was embarrassing. I can't believe I made that mistake (validating the feeling). But, I also wouldn't have discovered what I discovered without that mistake." If your child likes to read, you may find information about other scientists who chronicled their mistakes, thereby normalizing the process for her. In this way, we are using curiosity to help her actively expand her comfort zone for making mistakes. We want her to be aware of her own emotional profile, so it is helpful to be as explicit yet gentle as possible when you are working to address her vulnerabilities. By helping my child to reflect on her strengths, I am also helping her to:

- Build self-awareness;
- Create a toolbox of problem-solving strategies to use;
- Use passions and preferences to facilitate attention and engagement.

For example, if my child pays strict attention to details, then some of the things that he might be very good at would be building doll houses or miniatures of some kind. He may also be very good at cleaning, painting, accounting, or as a librarian. If my child has an intense interest in one area of study, then using a strengths-based framework, I may consider that my child can become a master and a leader in that field. They may become a docent at a museum or an entrepreneur. If my child is intensely focused on their own point of view, they may become a successful lawyer, lobbyist, and member of the debate team. There are many ways to reframe a particular strength and emotional profile. This is where we, as adults, may need to think outside of our comfort zones around what we consider typical. For a great read on this, check out Ken Robinson's *Finding Your Element,* a book about using your talents and passions to change your life outlook.

RUPTURE AND REPAIR

This all may sound wonderful and like the rest of your life is going to be a fairy tale if you are helping your child to be emotionally self-aware. However, things can and will go wrong. That's okay. Often, we will have a rupture in our relationship with our children when we are setting limits and creating and reinforcing boundaries. Children typically don't like to be told *no*. Frankly, adults don't like to be told *no*. However, we know that boundaries are necessary for safety and create a healthy framework for our children to work within. A very typical example of this is when you are at the store, your child asks for something, and you have to say no. The child becomes upset, but you know that children cannot have everything they want the instant they want it. We are mindful parents who want to instill delayed gratification, patience, and long-term thinking in our children. The child sees and wants because they are still impulsive. There is a disconnect, or a rupture, between our two frames of mind and our goals in that moment. With this rupture comes uncomfortable emotions for both of us. The child is angry or sad or both. We are frustrated, annoyed, embarrassed, or all of the above. We don't like these feelings, but we know they are necessary for us to tolerate so we can instill our long-term parental goals. So, as difficult as it may be, we stick to our guns.

It may ease your mind to know that we are not supposed to be in sync with our children all of the time. In his groundbreaking work, *The Neurobehavioral Relationships Between Parents and Infants,* Ed Tronik determined that parents and infants are typically only emotionally and cognitively in tune with each other about 30 percent of the time. When we are in sync with our children, we typically have the same goal in that moment; we are experiencing the same or similar emotions, and we notice that about each other.

When I am playing peek-a-boo with my child,

my only goal is to interact with her in a way that is engaging and fun for both of us. She enjoys it. I can tell because she makes eye contact with me, she smiles, and she is actively involved and anticipating my actions. I am in sync because I love the feeling it creates in me and in her. We keep going for a few minutes. At some point, doing the same action over and over loses its appeal. One or both of us may become bored and need additional stimulation or we may need a break from the interaction. I may look into the kitchen to see if my oven timer has gone off. That is a simple example of a rupture. We (mother and child) are no longer in sync with the same emotions and the same cognitive goal. One or the other can disengage or rupture the connection for a variety of reasons. This is typical and expected. It may be as simple as needing more, less, or different stimulation. It may be more complex, as when a parent needs to set boundaries causing the child to become upset. These ruptures will exist throughout the lifetime of our relationships. I personally breathed a huge sigh of relief when I learned that parents and children are typically only in sync 30 percent of the time. Knowing what can be reasonably expected allows us to be kinder to ourselves and to remove some of the judgment we place on our own skills and tolerance levels.

The repair occurs when we reengage, either around the original ideas and emotions or around something new. Perhaps in our previous example, mother and child don't play peek-a-boo again, they play something new like puppets. When both are feeling connected around the same idea and experiencing comfortable emotions, then a repair has happened. In our boundary-setting examples, the repair will likely occur a little while later, when the emotions are less intense. We may have a conversation with the child about our decisions. We may praise them for calming down after they were feeling upset. We may remind them about the toys they currently have and offer to play with them. The rupture and repair process is much like building a muscle. The relationship, like a muscle, must sometimes be broken down before it can be built back up to be something stronger.

TRY IT NOW

Notice several times this week when you have a rupture and repair with your child. Write down the details of the situation, and when you are calm and can be mindful, try to pull it apart. What were your goals in that moment? What were your child's goals? What emotions were you both feeling during the rupture? How did the repair happen: naturally, organically, or did one of you make a gesture to begin the repair process? Remember, this process is expected and helps to create stronger relationships moving forward.

7

INTERACT WITH PURPOSE

"Every person has a longing to be significant; to make a contribution; to be a part of something noble and purposeful."

— JOHN C. MAXWELL

Key Concepts:

- Interaction style
- Vulnerability
- Reframing

INTERACTION STYLE

The concepts and skills that we have talked about until now can easily be integrated into your everyday life. By simply tailoring the way that you interact with your child, you can bring in emotional language, self-reflection, and awareness around how emotions play a key role in our decisions. With some small changes to your interaction style, you can weave these ideas throughout every day.

One very simple but very powerful habit you can create is to begin every interaction with some emotional context. If you see that your child is playing with lots of movement and the characters are making sound effects, you may say, "Wow, that seems very *exciting*." Or if your child is outside swinging alone you may go out and ask, "Hey, are you feeling *lonely*?" In both examples, we are using a version of wondering about the emotional context of the situation. We used the word "seems" or we put our idea in the form of a question. We are not telling the child how they feel; we are creating the opportunity to collaborate about how the child is feeling. This is powerful in multiple ways. First, if you are correct, you're validating how the child feels. Feeling heard and understood is a core human need. Second, if you are not correct, you've just opened up the opportunity to have a conversation about how the child is actually feeling and what words they would use to describe their feelings. This is always where we want to start. We want to use the child's language as much as possible when we're having these conversations. What words do they use to describe how they are feeling?

Tommy threw a baseball at his sister after she came into his room and took some of his markers and paper without asking. Mom cannot allow her children to behave unsafely, however, Tommy does have valid feelings he is expressing in this situation. Mom starts by saying, "So, can you tell me what happened?" This alone is a non-judgmental way to begin. She is not scolding. She is not punishing. She is listening. Tommy feels like he can tell his side of the story openly and honestly. He says, "Molly is constantly going in my room without my permission and taking my stuff. She ruins my markers and then I don't have them to use when I want to work on my comic books. She never asks, she just takes. It's not fair." When Mom feels like she has heard the entire story from Tommy's perspective, beginning, middle, and end with relevant details included, she can then say, "So, let me see if I have this right...." or "So, what I hear you saying is...." Use a phrase that sits well with you but lets the child know that you are going to summarize what they just said, and you genuinely want to know if you understand them accurately. Mom might say, "So, what I hear you saying is that you feel like it is not fair (his word) when Molly comes into your room and takes your things without your permission. You feel frustrated (Mom's word) when she comes into your space and does not ask you if she can use your things. It definitely seems unfair for someone to take your things without your permission (validate the feelings). When you get frustrated, you may throw things at her (connecting feelings to behaviors). I wonder if you could do something different the next time you feel frustrated." We are modeling the notice and wonder process, without judgment, and creating space for them to take ownership of the solution.

Here is when you want to use your active listening skills. Do not underestimate the power of listening and exploring the child's perception of a situation. Listen to understand. Ask clarifying questions if you need to, but we are not interrupting. We are not problem-solving right now. We are not sharing our perspectives right now. Additionally, we are not checking our phones, smartwatches, the television, or multitasking. Allow your child to have your full attention during this time. They deserve it.

Next, we are going to reflect back to them what they said, as we understand it. As we're listening and reflecting with them, we should be using roughly 80 to 90 percent of the same words that they are using. The growth comes when we add just a little bit more to what they can already communicate. We may have a little bit of additional information to share that they didn't know. We may have slightly different language to add to help them build on their self-awareness and communication skills.

I once had to facilitate a situation where a child, we will call her Lucy, was very upset because two friends said they wouldn't play with her at recess. When it came time for them to go outside and play, Lucy did not know what to do. She wasn't very skilled at making friends or initiating play with other children. She was particularly comfortable with these two friends. So instead of letting them go out to the playground, she sat on both of them so they could not get away. You may know that sitting on your friends probably means that they're not going to be your friends for much longer. As I'm having a conversation with Lucy, she was able to tell me that she was feeling frustrated because her friends would not play with her on that day. I validated her feelings; I said I could understand why she was feeling frustrated about that situation. I did not condone the way that she handled it. However, I added one little thought to her perception of the situation. I said, "I wonder if you were also afraid that you would be lonely;" thinking consciously that anger is typically a secondary emotion, I wanted to bring in some other emotional possibilities. She sat up very straight, made direct eye contact with me, pointed at me, and said in a very excited tone, "Yes, that's it! I would be lonely if they don't play with me." Now, this was not the first time that she had heard the word lonely. She had heard this word and probably read this word before we had this conversation. However, in that moment, explicitly talking about it allowed her to connect that word with her internal experience. The word lonely was hers forever after that moment. So, instead of just saying, "I feel frustrated," she now can differentiate and use the word lonely when it's appropriate. This additional piece of vocabulary also helps her to facilitate a conversation with her friends. She's able to now say to them if you don't play with me, I will feel lonely. That is a very powerful way to use *I feel* statements. That doesn't mean that those friends will always play with her every day from then on. But it gives Lucy the power or the agency to represent her internal experience with a great degree of accuracy.

VULNERABILITY

Sometimes these conversations can be difficult when children are feeling vulnerable. Feelings of embarrassment and humiliation can be very difficult to discuss and to regulate. One strategy that works particularly well in that type of situation is using a third person. This can happen using action figures, stuffed animals, or beloved characters from a book. It is often much easier for a fragile, tender, or vulnerable ego to have conversations around those uncomfortable emotions when we can put the context into third person.

Once, back in high school, I had a paper to write. I waited until the last minute, rushed through it, and it was full of mistakes. When I got it back, it was full of red marks pointing out all of my spelling and grammatical error. At the top, my teacher had written "Fire your proofreader." Did he know that I waited until the last minute to do this paper? Of course, he did. Could he have said maybe next time you shouldn't wait till the last minute to do your work? Of course, he could have. But he knew that using a third person, my fictional proofreader, was a gentler way for him to convey his message. Rather than saying something that might be embarrassing or humiliating to me, I was able to "hear" and accept his corrective feedback without becoming defensive. He knew the goal was to change my behavior for the better, not to embarrass me.

From a parenting perspective, this could look like this: Mom walks into the bathroom to find shaving cream and shampoo all over the floor while Johnny is sitting right in the middle of it. He looks a little frightened when Mom appears, anticipating getting in trouble. What was the intention behind Johnny's actions here, from a purely developmental perspective? He was exploring the mechanics of the shaving cream bottle, the texture of the shaving cream and shampoo, viscosity as he mixed the two substances together, and gravity as he watched them fall to the floor. Mom sees a mess that she will have to clean up. However, after taking a few deep breaths and thinking like a three-year-old, Mom responds, "Boy, there must have been some busy scientists in here making experiments. I guess they were so excited about their results, they forgot to clean up." Johnny can now react in a number of ways that will protect his vulnerabilities. Importantly, he can choose how he wants to respond, creating a situation where he gets to think and analyze for himself. If he is relatively confident and proud of his actions, he may take credit for the mess and explain himself. He also has an out if he is feeling scared or embarrassed. He can join Mom in blaming the fictional scientists and then they can team up to clean up the mess, all the while reinforcing that they will have to remind the scientists to ask permission next time before undertaking such a full-scale experiment. This is not giving permission for the actions. It is a gentle way to have the conversation about mistakes and how to fix them in the future.

Another way to use daily interactions to help your children expand their emotional comfort zone and become more aware of their internal experiences is to begin to give emotions qualities and degrees. This goes back to that self-reflective process of thinking about the past, present, and future all at the same time. For example, you can help your child to notice that yesterday they seemed a bit grouchier than today. "I wonder if it was because you knew you needed to eat a snack in the middle of the morning. Tomorrow we'll be sure to have a snack ready to go so maybe you won't be grouchy at all." The idea is to work through the context of the situation using emotional language and highlighting the cause-and-effect process.

Eventually, you want to make these reflective timeframes longer and longer. You may say something like, "Last week when you waited until the last minute to do your homework, you felt anxious and disappointed in yourself. Next week, I wonder if there is a different way. Maybe I could help you to organize your time so that you feel productive and satisfied instead." Not only are we helping to expand the timeframe around which the child is reflecting, but in that example, we are replacing the uncomfortable emotions with the possibility of some comfortable emotions. These are simple but very powerful examples of daily opportunities we can create for emotional learning and self-reflection. If you are not used to doing this, it will take conscious practice and effort on your part and that's okay. It may be helpful for you to journal about how those interactions are making you feel. When it doesn't go well, it may make you feel inept, ineffective, foolish. How can you help yourself work through those emotions so that you can get back in there and keep trying?

REFRAMING

Additionally, we can help our children to consider different ways of looking at a situation by reframing it for them. This does not mean that we are invalidating their emotions. The feelings are valid no matter what. However, our perspective can really alter the way we manage those emotions. In schools, we often talk about a growth mindset or the power of "yet." We support our students to think about mistakes and missteps as part of the learning process, which they are. However, some children see mistakes as failure that brings with it accompanying embarrassment or humiliation. No one wants to feel embarrassed or humiliated, so we will often avoid situations that we anticipate may bring about those emotions. In some children, this can cultivate a habit of avoiding risks altogether and/ or becoming perfectionists. Going down this path leads to more uncomfortable emotions. These children feel anxious, have a strong need to control every situation, and generally have a low tolerance for anything outside their comfort zones. We can help them reframe these situations by helping them to see that struggle is a natural part of learning and life. We can model reframing with a sentence like "So, another way to think about this could be...." Be explicit; convey times when you struggled, and then achieved your goal. Talk about what you can do during times of struggle, such as stay calm, break the problem down into smaller parts, take a break and come back, evaluate your resources, and ask clarifying questions. Taking action, almost any action, helps us to feel powerful and reduce stress. As we help our children to reframe how they are thinking about stressful situations, we are expanding their comfort zones and their abilities to self-regulate. The counterbalance of a perfectionist mind frame is flexible thinking, persistence, and a willingness to think creatively. Most parents strive for their children to possess these qualities.

TRY IT NOW

Choose one or two situations and help your child reflect on the emotions they experienced during that time. Help them make connections between what caused the emotion (past), how it felt in the moment – include feeling words and intensity level (present) – and how they might handle the same situation in the future (future). This process is the core of reflective thinking. It may take practice or seem awkward at first, and that is okay. Our reflective skills are typically developed in hindsight at first before we can consciously notice what we are feeling in the moment. Accurate self-reflection is a skill that needs lots of practice before you or your child will feel like it comes naturally.

8

FIND YOUR INNER CHILD

"Accepting your playful side is actually inner power being released. Playfulness is powerful."

— G. J. REYNOLDS

Key Concepts:

- Range of emotions – revisited
- Playfulness
- Power

RANGE OF EMOTIONS – REVISITED

"Development, it turns out, occurs through this process of progressively more complex exchanges between a child and somebody else – especially somebody who's crazy about that child," says Urie Bronfenbrenner, the founder of Head Start, an early intervention program that provides education, nutrition, and parent training in the United States. This is where we begin. You are that person for your child. Our job is to support our children to believe that their ideas are fabulous! Big ideas, small ideas, and everything in between. This is true whether we are joining them in play, engaging in daily common interactions, assisting them with homework, or helping them heal from heartbreak. Crafting our interactions to support our little ones – or not so little ones – to believe that their ideas are fantastic goes well beyond self-esteem. When our children believe that they have important ideas to share, they're much more willing to persist, take risks, and communicate at a complex level. So, let's take a step back and discuss how to decide what this looks like.

We've talked about taking a critical look at your child's emotional profile. Right now, today, what emotions is my child comfortable with, uncomfortable with, and what is their tolerance level for all of those? Now we're going to connect this with the dreams that we have for them. Compare that emotional profile of where they are now to where they would need to be to achieve those dreams. The distance between those two points is what is going to guide our decision-making as parents. When do we push boundaries or when do we pull back and support and join? Depending on the discipline you're talking about, there are lots of ways to describe the sweet spot of learning. This is the place where the child is engaging in activities that are somewhat challenging yet achievable. They can struggle a bit, persist through that struggle, and feel the pride of success when they work through and achieve their goal. In educational terms, Vygotsky called it the Zone of Proximal Development. It is our job to be aware of where that sweet spot is for our children. Sometimes we will need to co-regulate with them to pull them back into that zone. Other times we will need to challenge them to push them into that zone. Playfulness can be the solution in both situations.

Consider this example, my daughter is building a castle with blocks. Perhaps she becomes frustrated when she cannot build it as tall as she would like. I can join her as a construction specialist and make some suggestions for how the castle could be more structurally sound, using language that makes sense to her. In this example, I am co-regulating with her by joining the play, confirming that her idea of building the castle is, of course, fabulous, and then helping her achieve that goal.

On the other hand, perhaps, she builds a simple castle quite quickly but then does not know how to expand the play from there and becomes bored and disengaged. I can join the play as a dragon who needs a much bigger place to sleep and give her some specific suggestions for adding complexity to the castle. The sweet spot is a goal that perfectly blends something that is challenging (resulting in feelings of excitement and power) and achievable (resulting in feelings of pride and satisfaction). While we know that children must experience uncomfortable emotions throughout life, supporting them to be in the sweet spot helps them internalize some of the comfortable emotions and then build successful habits such as self-reflection, persistence, and responsible risk-taking.

PLAYFULNESS

Let's look at some examples. Imagine I'm watching my daughter write a fictional story. Throughout this process, she is asking me very often how to spell a word. The teacher prefers that the students listen for the sounds that are in the words and use invented spelling because they are critically engaging with letters and text through that process. She is more focused on the process of learning to spell rather than a correct answer. My daughter, however, is very uncomfortable with the idea of possibly making a mistake. She does not want to be wrong. She anticipates that that will make her feel embarrassed and humiliated, even if she is not aware of this on a conscious level. So, fear of feeling embarrassed is stifling her writing and her ideas. She cannot allow a free flow of ideas in her writing for fear of spelling a word wrong.

As I'm evaluating her emotional profile, I would say to myself she is uncomfortable and/ or fearful of feeling embarrassed. This causes anxiety and blocks her flow of ideas. What can I do to counterbalance that? How can I support her to reframe her thinking so that she can consider mistakes a natural and acceptable part of learning? Playfulness. I found the biggest piece of cardboard I could find and drew an eraser on it. You know those pink, oblong erasers we all had in elementary school? I drew it, colored it, cut it out and gave it to her. It was larger than my torso. I told her that no matter how big a mistake she made, we could always find an eraser big enough to change it. She laughed and understood my point. This does not mean we can dismiss her feelings. Her fear of feeling embarrassed is very real, personal, and valid. However, she now has a slightly bigger framework for thinking about it. It is not black-and-white, do-or-die. There is a gray area where we can make changes, learn, and grow.

The same idea can be used with younger children who have less experience and will need more support as they learn and grow. We still want them thinking for themselves, but we will need to scaffold some ideas for them a bit more than older children. For little people, it can be helpful to offer multiple choices, one that is realistic and one that is absolutely ridiculous. They still get to do the thinking because they are making a choice, but they also get the confidence that comes with knowing they probably made the best choice. For example, if your child is trying to open the toy box and cannot get it open, you could ask them what do you want out of the toy box, your truck or a banana? It is okay for us to ask them questions even when we already know what the answer is. By scaffolding them in this way, they are allowed the opportunity to think, choose, and communicate their ideas. Earlier I talked about being careful using why questions. Using multiple-choice is a very powerful strategy for supporting kids to be able to accurately answer why questions and think critically about their thinking. Going back to our toy box example, "Why do you want the truck out of the toy box? Do you want to drive or eat it?" It is a silly question; however, it's a very simple approach that creates a situation where our children feel the power of thinking for themselves and successfully communicating their ideas. There is an unlimited number of ways to apply the playfulness principle to your interactions. Be cautious that you do not come across as being dismissive or flippant. The purpose of these playful interactions is to support our children to express their valid and fabulous ideas. We are merely facilitators joining in their wonderful world.

POWER

I have talked about power and agency several times. It is extremely important from a developmental perspective that children are comfortable feeling powerful and assertive. Not only will this support them to be more confident expressing their ideas, but it can also be necessary for their safety. Unfortunately, many of our children will fall into a category that makes them more vulnerable than other children. These children are statistically significantly more likely to be victimized. It is important that one part of the range of emotions we prioritize is feeling powerful. Learning to communicate your ideas also includes being able to protest. As parents, we often find protest annoying and inconvenient. However, we do need our children to be able to protest. We want them to notice when something doesn't feel right. They have got to be able to say no, to understand that they have control over their body and no one else does. You can model this for them during play with more everyday types of exchanges. For example, your daughter wants your horse to go over to the ranch and pick up the cowboys or cowgirls. Unfortunately, you have to inform her that your horse isn't feeling good today and she really has to go lay down right now. Maybe later she'll be feeling better and can help at the ranch. Now, this is a very minor example, however, it is modeling the idea that we can listen to our bodies and we can say no. Another way to allow your child to experience power and control is by sitting below your child's eye level during interactions. That is a nonverbal way of handing power over to the person who is physically in a taller position. It's an energy exchange that your child will come to feel as being powerful.

What if I'm not good at being playful? It's been a long time since I've been a kid. That's okay. Practice letting go of your comfort zone and your pride for the sake of your child's development. Be silly, be ridiculous, be off the wall. If you're having a hard time, have someone video record you and watch the videos back. As you're watching, consider opportunities where you could have been more playful. Consider opportunities where you may have said something just slightly differently that would have ensured you were following your child's ideas or your child's intentions. There's a good chance this will make you feel awkward and uncomfortable. If you were super confident in your parenting skills, you wouldn't be reading this book. So, it's okay to allow yourself to feel awkward and uncomfortable so that you can use that exercise for self-reflection and improvement. Watching video recordings is a fantastic way to notice tiny shifts in thinking and emotional tone. it can really help you to learn to listen with more than your ears.

TRY IT NOW

Go for it! Be playful, silly, ridiculous in your play and interaction with your children this week. Set aside your parent brain, your pride, your embarrassment, and be playful. Crawl, jump, play, hide, sing, dress up. Give them the gift of you in a silly state. Notice how it feels to you but also how they respond. Likely, you will see that their emotional engagement increases during this time.

9

YIELD TO THE GRAY

"Compassion, tolerance, forgiveness, and a sense of self-discipline are qualities that help us lead our daily lives with a calm mind."

— DALAI LAMA

Key Concepts:

- Opportunity cost
- Rupture and repair – revisited
- Peace not perfection

OPPORTUNITY COST

Up to this point, we've been discussing the importance of supporting our kids to be able to express and tolerate a wide range of emotions. Let's flip the coin and think about what it would be like if we don't allow them to experience uncomfortable emotions, or emotions that are uncomfortable to me as the parent or caregiver. Most reflecting begins with the parent. If we are not supporting our children to express certain emotions or certain intensity levels, it is typically because we are uncomfortable with them. Consider what types of people may have difficulty accomplishing this. If my personality tends to be calm, quiet, and focused, and I'm not a real woohoo kind of person, then being big and silly is probably going to feel very unnatural for me. And if my child is expressing an intense emotion – be it comfortable or uncomfortable – then I may struggle to stay regulated and remain engaged with the interaction.

The opposite could also be true. If my personality is big, bold, and loud but my child prefers quieter, softer types of interactions, then it may be off-putting for my child. She may disengage with the interaction because it's hard for her to stay regulated with our mismatched profiles. This will happen. It's okay. Remember you're only supposed to be in sync approximately 30 percent of the time.

But go back to the foundations. We want to support our children to feel pride, curiosity, power, assertiveness, sadness, disappointment, and the list goes on. If we do not allow them to struggle and feel disappointed, we are also taking away their opportunity to feel proud and successful when they persevere through a problem. If we do not support them to fully explore their curiosity, then we are denying them the opportunity to feel satisfied that they have made a discovery.

My youngest daughter was mixing paint in two bags filled with shaving cream. She added some blue paint and some yellow paint and mixed it together to get green. She asked me if that happens every time. I suggested she keep trying in order to find that out for herself. So, bag after bag she put blue and yellow paint together. Every time it made green, but she was able to make that determination for herself. She conducted that experiment enough times to make her feel satisfied that blue + yellow = green is a constant. She took the action, she did the thinking, and she drew the conclusion. This is handing the power over to the child. I noticed what her idea was, joined and validated her curiosity, and supplied her with the necessary materials (and moral support) to complete her experiment.

RUPTURE AND REPAIR – REVISITED

There will be times when we are not in sync with our children. This is natural and expected. It is through this breakdown and buildup that our relationships deepen. Much like the fibers in a muscle must be broken down before they can be built back up even stronger, relationships must go through the same process. We must keep our children safe, and we must help them to understand boundaries. These circumstances often cause a rupture. Children and parents may become angry, upset, and sad during these interactions.

Visualize: You walk into the kitchen to find your child has taken every pot and pan out of the cupboard and created a host of musical instruments. You could be curious and join them in their musical endeavor, however, you have twenty minutes to get dinner ready before a conference call. You are already feeling stressed about the call because you don't feel prepared. You see the mess and it pushes you past your frustration tolerance. You yell, "Clean this up right now!" Your child is startled and begins to cry. Your feelings are valid in this moment. However, you ruptured the relationship with your impulsive outburst. It is now your job to repair the relationship by restoring the emotional connection. You can achieve this through apologizing, soothing, and comforting your child. It is important to model apologizing when it is appropriate. This is a major tool in starting the repair process. It is important to remember to be accepting of both the child and ourselves here. There is no judgment. We are both doing the best we can to navigate the uncomfortable but necessary disengagement in our duo. In *Parenting from the Inside Out,* Dan Siegel, M.D. and Mary Hartzell, M. Ed. devote an entire chapter to discussing why this process is a necessary step in deepening and strengthening relationships.

PEACE NOT PERFECTION

Eventually, we want to become parents who feel at peace about their parenting decisions. We will never be perfect parents. That is okay, we aren't supposed to be. Parenting is a journey where the caregivers learn just as much, if not more, about themselves, the world, and life than we teach our children. If we can feel confident that we are focusing on the foundational knowledge and skills that will lead our children to be happy and healthy adults, then we can find peace, even in our mistakes. We are able to create a space for growth, creativity, risk-taking, curiosity, uncomfortable feelings, and grace for ourselves and our children. This is the ultimate parenting goal.

TRY IT NOW

Evaluate two parenting situations this week: one you think went well and one you think went poorly. Begin your reflection with this piece of self-talk:

"I entered this situation with good intentions, the best information I currently have, love for my child, and love for myself."

Now, begin your reflection. What emotions and with what intensity were you both feeling? Did I consciously consider my child's emotional state first and foremost? What strategies did I try to use: validating feelings, mirroring, counterbalancing? Did I distract us away from the intense feelings or did I support us to both stay in the moment so we could work through it together? Did I react impulsively? Could I do something differently next time that would create a better result? There are no right or wrong answers to these questions. They are meant to be a framework for helping you to kindly and gently reflect on your thinking through specific instances, so that you can improve the next time. Remember, we all have room for growth, all of us. Be kind to yourself as you go through the process.

10

WHEN IT DOESN'T GO AS PLANNED

"The most valuable thing you can make is a mistake – you can't learn anything from being perfect."

— ADAM OSBORNE

Key Concepts:

- Taking ownership
- Reinforcement systems
- Reflective practices

TAKING OWNERSHIP

If you have made it this far, you probably are now invested in the ideas and skills described in the previous chapters. You may have already tried putting some of the ideas in place. Hopefully, you are excited to have a framework to support your parenting goals, a framework that helps you build an emotional foundation that your family can build on for the rest of their lives. By now you will have begun to practice each of these steps of the *notice and wonder* cycle. You are noticing what is happening inside your body and the physical reactions that precede and correspond with more intense emotions. You are expanding the language that you use to express your emotions and you're helping your child to do the same. Once you have noticed and labeled the emotions, then you can decide what action you want to take in response to them. The space between labeling your emotion and deciding what you want to do is the place where impulsivity is replaced by self-reflection and reasoning. This is the ultimate goal as we learn to practice self-regulation and move our children from co-regulation to having agency over their emotions.

In an ideal world, we will go through this process

successfully multiple times a day. Our emotional range will expand, and our comfort zones will get wider. We will become more adaptable and better able to effectively handle whatever the world brings our way. However, we all live in the real world. There will be days when we don't want to be self-reflective, when we don't feel like being adaptable, when we just are not the right person to bring calm into our children's chaos. And that's okay. I have many examples of days like these in my past and, I'm sure, in my future.

One of the more memorable times was when I was trying to mediate between two twelve-year-old boys. They were having a very difficult time working collaboratively with each other. They both felt very strongly that their idea was the best idea and neither of them wanted to compromise. One boy said to me, "I don't want to use his idea," And I thought to myself, "Well, I don't want to drive a minivan, but sometimes we have to do things we don't want to do." I could have said that out loud, but it probably would not have fostered open self-reflection or led the boys to be more collaborative. But that's real life.

There will be days when you will use the ideas and strategies from this book and your children will make tremendous personal and emotional progress. There will be days when the whole thing is an absolute train wreck. Both of those outcomes are okay if we continue to be self-reflective, open to improvements, and to move on to the next letter in the alphabet. There will be days when it's hard. And that's okay too. I almost relish it more when my children say to me, "But this is hard," and I say, "Yes, it is and that's okay because we can do hard things." Not *I* can do hard things, or *you* can do hard things, but *we* can do hard things. We are in this together – we are a team – when things go well and when things go poorly. You will need adult support through this process. You will need someone to wonder with you. Think seriously about a variety of people who can help you in this area. There is no one right way to go about this but you need to have someone to wonder with.

REINFORCEMENT SYSTEMS

You may decide you want a more systematic process for helping you and your children to remember the process of notice, wonder, label, and decide. You may think it's a good idea to put a reward system in place. Perhaps you decide, every time my child accurately labels their emotion, they get a sticker. We will hang this sticker chart on the refrigerator. For every ten stickers, they get an ice cream cone. A formal process with visual reminders can be helpful for some people especially when they are first beginning to establish a habit. However, I would caution you against the idea of a reward system. It may be helpful at the very beginning, but it will quickly lose its effectiveness and here's why: a reinforcement system focuses on surface behaviors. Our goal is to teach our children to focus on their internal experiences. We want them to be able to listen to their bodies and use the information that they hear to help them make the best decisions that they can. Yes, this is much harder than focusing on the things that we can see our children do or say.

However, if you're going to make the effort to teach the concepts in this book to your child, you want it to be deeply and lastingly effective. Our brains have already created a reward system that they are quite proud of. Feelings of pride, success, accomplishment, and satisfaction – comfortable emotions – tell us that our actions were successful, that we should repeat those actions. Conversely, feeling embarrassment, regret, or sadness is typically an uncomfortable experience and we learn that we do not want to experience those. This creates an *approach* (do things that will help me recreate the comfortable emotions) and *avoid* (do not do the things that created the uncomfortable emotions) pattern for our brains. The reward is this sense of pride telling us we made good choices. The reward is feeling joy or excitement after taking a risk to ride that very scary roller coaster and then to find out that we loved it. The reward is the internal experience when we feel genuinely connected to someone else. Those are the rewards that we need to help our children to learn to notice and then to assistance them to reflect on what they mean and what they are telling us.

We are born with an internal reward system. It is our job to give our children the words, the understanding, and the processes to notice this internal reward system and apply it effectively throughout their lives. We may gently help our children to reflect after a successful endeavor. They worked hard to be able to earn a yellow belt, play a sonata, spell all the -un words. We need to explicitly point out the actions they took and the feelings that resulted, connecting actions to behaviors. "Wow, you worked so hard to learn that song on the piano. You played it without any mistakes! You must be so proud of yourself. The next time you have a new song, I bet you will practice the same way you did for this song." We are making the intrinsic explicit through our narrative of their actions. We are also helping them to see the past, the present, and the future, all at the same time. Holding these ideas at the same time is the foundation of our reflective practices.

Please no stickers!

REFLECTIVE PRACTICES

Throughout the book, I have talked about some practices that you can put in place to help you reflect on your own emotions, your child's emotions, and your interaction choices. One of the most powerful is video recording either yourself with your child or your child alone. Watching back a video recording allows you to take a step back from the situation and think about it almost from the view of an outsider. It allows you the time to notice nuances that you may not when you are in the moment, having an interaction with your child. But this is just one method of self-reflection. You do need other adults to wonder with you. We all have those friends we trust who won't judge us and who will tell us honestly how they feel. We need those friends who will call us out on our baloney: those friends who will tell you when you're making excuses, when you're not being honest with yourself, or when you're just plain wrong. We also need those friends to boost us up, tell us that we are doing a great job, and that we are enough. I once had a mentor say that sometimes it is enough just to show up. At the time, I thought that was a pretty low standard. However, through my own journey of self-reflection, wondering, and learning to release judgment, I now wholeheartedly agree that sometimes it is enough just to show up.

All that being said, however, sometimes we need more professional levels of reflective practices. For us to really grow, we need to interact with people who know more than we do, who have a wider range of experience than we do, and who can see much farther into the future with a broader perspective for the present. I encourage you to make those types of connections. You never want to be the smartest person in the room. You always want there to be someone there that you can learn and grow from. There are lots of opportunities for this type of reflective support in person and online. There will be times when you are just stuck. You try a bunch of strategies and do not get the outcome you want. You may have stressors and triggers in your life that take an emotional toll on you, leaving little left for your family. This is real life. I encourage you to find a tribe that gets you, validates you and your efforts, but also expands your skills and thinking. They are out there, and they probably also read this book.

Please join our online forum as an additional place for you to get support, feedback, and validation. We have a group of people who come together, knowing that it is a safe space to be vulnerable but also a group who understands the magnitude of your parenting victories. Parents can share their stories, ask for advice, offer support to each other. We share tips on many aspects of parenting to help you continue your journey with information, best intentions, and self-love. Join us!

TRY IT NOW

Allow yourself to be vulnerable. Find a group of people with whom you can share your vulnerabilities: people who will listen, validate, commiserate, and lift you up without judgment. We can do hard things but not always by ourselves.

11

YOUR FAMILY DESERVES THE BEST YOU

Imagine this: Cara walks down the stairs and her children are playing with Legos together. Luke yells at Sarah, "Hey, I was playing with that one."

Sarah says, "Sorry, Luke, I didn't know you were using that one. Here you go."

"Thanks, Sis. I'm sorry I yelled at you. I was really into building and not thinking about what you needed for your project. Want to put them together and make something even bigger?"

Cara thinks, wow, that was a beautiful interaction between them. They expressed their emotions and acknowledged each other's feeling as well as their own roles in the situation. They even worked together to create something bigger than their own ideas! Put that one in the win column!

Let's recap how Cara got there. She achieved her own peace and her children's ability to articulate their feelings by trying the ideas presented here and then reflecting with me afterward. We would wonder together about the times that went well and when things went poorly. There will be victories, train wrecks, and everything in between. She was able to remain peaceful in her decisions because she knew she was keeping these fundamental ideas in mind:

- Consciously considering her children's emotional world
- Reflecting on her own emotional profile
- Noticing and wondering without judgment
- Using strategies to support co-regulation like mirroring and counterbalancing
- Supporting her children to experience, tolerate, and eventually regulate a wide range of emotions
- Acknowledging her assumptions about a situation
- Considering how her children can use

their strengths to support times when they are vulnerable

- Giving herself grace by accepting that rupture and repair are expected in all relationships; in fact, when handled well, actually strengthen relationships
- Becoming more playful
- Considering a different way of doing things

You can have these wins and they will continue throughout your children's lives when you focus on their internal emotional worlds. You may raise a child who is comfortable being assertive and confident enough to apply for every possible scholarship, setting herself up for a stress-free (at least financially) undergraduate career. You may raise a child who starts a Gay-Straight Alliance group at her high school because she wants to create a safe space for a vulnerable group of people. Your children will achieve things you never thought possible or even considered because you taught them to be bold and to regulate the uncomfortable feelings that come with that. You taught them to be empathetic and to anticipate the possible downfalls of putting yourself out there. You taught them to manage a range of emotions so that they can take risks, change their world for the better, feel pride in their success, and handle sadness and disappointment with grace.

You want to be your best. As a parent, you want to be equally rested, energetic, empathetic, creative, organized, validating, and playful, among many other things. We try until we are exhausted. We know that is not the best of us. We set achievable goals for ourselves and our families, yet we still fall short. Focusing on our emotional profile, our children's emotional profile, releasing judgment, reflecting, and purposefully bringing joy to our lives fills our bucket, fortifies our nervous system, and sets us up for success. We are better able to tolerate and regulate intense, uncomfortable emotions. This is the ultimate parenting goal and the ultimate human goal. Keep practicing, make mistakes, get support, and you will reach the heights you set for yourself and your family. You are not alone. We can do hard things.

ABOUT THE AUTHOR

Dr. Christine Harkness has a PhD in Infant and Early Childhood Development. She is a parent coach and special education teacher. Over the last twenty-five years, she has supported hundreds of parents and caregivers to improve their relationships with their children.

Christine integrates concepts of emotional intelligence, play therapy, and trauma practice to help families understand a child's emotional world. She teaches reflective practices, self-awareness, and simple shifts in ways of interacting within the context of the caregiver/ child partnership.

Christine is a Therapeutic Crisis Intervention trainer. Her work with children in crisis has helped her to be acutely attuned to the emotional states of children and adults. She loves to incorporate body and breathwork into her practices as a Breath, Body, and Mind Level Two coach. The body has an amazing ability to heal itself under some very simple circumstances.

Based on her knowledge as a DIR/Floortime Expert Training Leader, Christine founded Magic Moments, a summer camp for children who needed extra practice relating and communicating. For five years, she paired children who were vulnerable in these areas with typically developing same-aged peers as their play partners. Therapeutic adult play counselors would help the pairs to play, communicate, problem-solve, and blend their ideas in a natural environment.

Christine is raising two beautiful daughters. Her

daughters have a strong moral compass and work hard to support social justice issues. She is newly married, loving life, and sharing her passions with families who want to embody calm, peaceful parenting.

ABOUT DIFFERENCE PRESS

Difference Press is the exclusive publishing arm of The Author Incubator, an educational company for entrepreneurs – including life coaches, healers, consultants, and community leaders – looking for a comprehensive solution to get their books written, published, and promoted. Its founder, Dr. Angela Lauria, has been bringing to life the literary ventures of hundreds of authors-in-transformation since 1994.

A boutique-style self-publishing service for clients of The Author Incubator, Difference Press boasts a fair and easy-to-understand profit structure, low-priced author copies, and author-friendly contract terms. Most importantly, all of our #incubatedauthors maintain ownership of their copyright at all times.

LET'S START A MOVEMENT WITH YOUR MESSAGE

In a market where hundreds of thousands of books are published every year and are never heard from again, The Author Incubator is different. Not only do all Difference Press books reach Amazon bestseller status, but all of our authors are actively changing lives and making a difference.

Since launching in 2013, we've served over 500 authors who came to us with an idea for a book and were able to write it and get it self-published in less than 6 months. In addition, more than 100 of those books were picked up by traditional publishers and are now available in bookstores. We do this by selecting the highest quality and highest potential applicants for our future programs.

Our program doesn't only teach you how to write a book – our team of coaches, developmental editors, copy editors, art directors, and marketing experts incubate you from having a book idea to being a published, bestselling author, ensuring that the book you create can actually make a difference in the world. Then we give you the training you need to use your book to make the difference in the world, or to create a business out of serving your readers.

ARE YOU READY TO MAKE A DIFFERENCE?

You've seen other people make a difference with a book. Now it's your turn. If you are ready to stop watching and start taking massive action, go to http://theauthorincubator.com/apply/.

"Yes, I'm ready!"

OTHER BOOKS BY DIFFERENCE PRESS

Skinny Genes: The Surprising Truth about Every Body's Capacity to Settle at a Natural Weight, Even When Diets Have Failed by Arianne Bozarth, CNS, MS

Family Business Legacy Plan: The Ultimate Guide to Creating a Legacy for Your Family without Paying too Much in Taxes by Maria L. Ellis, MBA

iMove: Helping Your Clients Heal from Compulsive Exercise by Amy Gardner, MS, CERD, RYT

Rising Beyond Betrayal: One Woman's Guest for Peace after Tragedy, Trauma, and Loss by Lise-Marie Monroe

The Essential Oil Business: A Heart-Centered Entrepreneur's Guide to Adding a New Stream of Revenue by Lori Rothschild, PhD

True Gifts: Ignite Your Soul Magic and Monetize the Highest Expression of Your Purpose by Jewel Veitch

No More Playing Small: Free Your Inner Rockstar and Go All in on Your Full-Time Coaching Career by Megan Jo Wilson

THANK YOU

Thank you so much for reading *Calm Mom: Tips and Tricks to Stop Yelling, Stay Calm, and Raise Happy, Healthy Kids.* The personal journey we take as parents is one of the most rewarding and difficult aspects of our lives. Your children will reap the benefits of your willingness to be vulnerable and reflective in order to become a better parent. Congratulations!

If you would like to continue deepening your parenting journey, I am offering a free class that expands on the ideas in the book. If you would like the link for the free class, email me at drchristineharkness@gmail.com.

I would love to learn more about your parenting journey, dreams for your children, victories, and vulnerabilities. Please keep in touch on Facebook @drchristineharkness. We have a brilliant group of parents who come together to share their stories and support one another. You are welcome with open arms!

Made in the USA
Columbia, SC
18 September 2022